T0209793

How Real is God?

Donya Gonzalez

Copyright © 2022 Donya Gonzalez.

All rights reserved. No part of this book may be used or reproduced by any means, graphic, electronic, or mechanical, including photocopying, recording, taping or by any information storage retrieval system without the written permission of the author except in the case of brief quotations embodied in critical articles and reviews.

This book is a work of non-fiction. Unless otherwise noted, the author and the publisher make no explicit guarantees as to the accuracy of the information contained in this book and in some cases, names of people and places have been altered to protect their privacy.

WestBow Press books may be ordered through booksellers or by contacting:

WestBow Press
A Division of Thomas Nelson & Zondervan
1663 Liberty Drive
Bloomington, IN 47403
www.westbowpress.com
844-714-3454

Because of the dynamic nature of the Internet, any web addresses or links contained in this book may have changed since publication and may no longer be valid. The views expressed in this work are solely those of the author and do not necessarily reflect the views of the publisher, and the publisher hereby disclaims any responsibility for them.

Any people depicted in stock imagery provided by Getty Images are models, and such images are being used for illustrative purposes only.
Certain stock imagery © Getty Images.

ISBN: 978-1-6642-5661-3 (sc)
ISBN: 978-1-6642-5692-7 (e)

Library of Congress Control Number: 2022902264

Print information available on the last page.

WestBow Press rev. date: 02/25/2022

WESTBOW
PRESS®
A DIVISION OF THOMAS NELSON
& ZONDERVAN

How Real is God?

Dedication

● ○ ● ●

For my dad, whose amazing love made me dream amazingly. Love you always.

Also, to my dear friend and sister in Christ, J.J., thank you for being my cheerleader, my sounding board, and for your encouragement. I will be forever grateful for your love and support.

How real is God? He is as real as the laugh that comes up from your belly and out of your mouth!

4

He's as real as the tears that
fall from your eyes when you fall
down and scrape your knee.

He's as real as the butterfly
that kisses your finger.

He's as real as a raindrop that falls from the sky to splash against your cheek.

He's as real as a snowflake that floats from the sky and lands on your tongue.

12

He's as real as the hug from mommy
or daddy when you feel sad.

He's as real as the special kiss
on the forehead from grandma
when she comes to visit.

He's as real as the wind that stirs up
the leaves on a windy Fall day.

How real is God? Look in the mirror,
He's as real as you and me!

Printed in the United States
by Baker & Taylor Publisher Services